Beautifully Broken

Because healing isn't forgetting — it's remembering and choosing to survive anyway!

Miss Tiramisu, Once His Home

India | USA | UK

Copyright © Miss Tiramisu, Once His Home
All Rights Reserved.

This book has been self-published with all reasonable efforts taken to make the material error-free by the author. No part of this book shall be used, reproduced in any manner whatsoever without written permission from the author, except in the case of brief quotations embodied in critical articles and reviews.

The Author of this book is solely responsible and liable for its content including but not limited to the views, representations, descriptions, statements, information, opinions, and references ["Content"]. The Content of this book shall not constitute or be construed or deemed to reflect the opinion or expression of the Publisher or Editor. Neither the Publisher nor Editor endorse or approve the Content of this book or guarantee the reliability, accuracy, or completeness of the Content published herein and do not make any representations or warranties of any kind, express or implied, including but not limited to the implied warranties of merchantability, fitness for a particular purpose.

The Publisher and Editor shall not be liable whatsoever...

Made with ❤ on the BookLeaf Publishing Platform
www.bookleafpub.in
www.bookleafpub.com

Dedication

To the ones who loved too deeply,
who stayed when they should've walked away,
who kept choosing to love even when it didn't choose them back.
To every heart that broke — but didn't stop beating.
This is for you.
May you always remember — even broken things can still shine.

Preface

This book wasn't planned.
It was written in the quiet hours between heartbreak and healing —
in the middle of tears, silence, and long nights that refused to end.
I didn't write it to be brave; I wrote it to survive.
Each chapter came from something I lived,
something I felt too deeply to keep inside.

If you've ever loved and lost — this book is your mirror.
It won't tell you to move on.
It will simply sit beside you in your ache
and remind you that you are not alone.
Because love, loss, and healing — they're not opposites.
They're the same story, told in different seasons.

So, take a deep breath, turn the page slowly,
and let yourself feel everything.
Maybe, by the end, you'll realize
you were never broken. You were just becoming.

Acknowledgements

To every person who became a chapter —
thank you, even if you never meant to stay.
You taught me what love is,
what it isn't,
and what I am capable of surviving.

To the friends who listened to the same story a hundred times —
thank you for never asking me to stop telling it.

To my family — for loving me through the silence.

And to the readers —
thank you for holding these words the way I once held him —
carefully, completely, and with hope.

And to the girl I used to be —
you thought this was the end, didn't you?
But this — this was your beginning.
You weren't broken.
You were being rewritten by the universe itself.

Chapter 1. After It Ended

Some heartbreaks don't scream, they fade, quietly, like they never happened
They die in half-typed texts left on "seen"
in silence that becomes habit.
No big fights, no closure — just a slow fading,
like light slowly leaving a room.

People think I've moved on.
But they don't see how gentle I've become with myself —
how I carry my heart like it could break any moment,
how one small memory is still enough to shake my whole world.

They say time heals.
Maybe it does — but not the way we think.
Sometimes it doesn't fix the hurt —
it just teaches you how to live with it.
How to smile like nothing broke inside you.
How to hear their favorite song and not skip it.

I don't just miss *you*.
I miss *me* —
the girl who believed love could fix everything.
Now she knows love can leave without reason,

and still somehow, you survive.

I can do the little things again —
walk past your favorite aisle,
fold my clothes in silence.
Maybe that's healing…
or maybe it's just me learning to live with it,
because what else can I do?

It doesn't come all at once.
It slips in softly —
in the middle of an ordinary day.

The cracks are still there,
but they don't sting now.
They just shine quietly,
as if they've accepted their place.
Maybe that's what love does —
it destroys you just enough
to show you the beauty in what remains.

Chapter 2. After the Ringing Stops

When love ends, no one tells you what comes next.
The world doesn't pause for your heartbreak.
The sun still rises, people still laugh,
and you still wake up with that same heavy heart —
wondering how to live a life that suddenly feels too quiet.

The phone doesn't ring anymore.
At first, you wait.
You stare at it, check the screen again and again,
telling yourself maybe they're busy, maybe they're upset,
maybe they're waiting for *you* to call first.

You replay that last goodbye —
the way they said, *"talk to you later,"*
and you didn't know that *later* meant *never.*

People said, "Just block him. Delete everything."
But I couldn't.
Not because I wanted him to come back —
but because pretending he never existed
felt like lying to my own past.

Some nights, I still talk to him in my head.
Not to fix anything,
just to remember how my voice sounded
when I still believed in love.
The words come softer now,
like I'm speaking to a memory that's tired of being
helpless, tired of being stuck.

I used to think closure meant a message —
one last call, one clean goodbye,
something that would make the pain make sense.
But closure doesn't come from people.
It comes from truth —
the kind that breaks you first,
the kind you fight with everything in you.

You cry, you beg, you wait.
You do everything for them to come back —
to call, to say sorry, even when it wasn't your fault.
And when nothing works, you stop trying —
and that's when you realize…
you don't move on — **you just survive it.**

Chapter 3. What's Left of Me

I thought I would feel free.
But the truth was quieter than that.

I woke up the next morning and everything looked the same — my room, my phone, even my face in the mirror — yet nothing felt like mine anymore.

I went to work like usual.
Smiled at people.
Answered messages with emojis that didn't mean anything.

I'd pick my outfit and still think, *he liked this color.*
I'd pour my morning chai and smile — it was never as good as his.
I'd laugh at something funny, then suddenly stop — because for a second, I wished he could've heard it too.
That's how heartbreak hides — not in the crying, but in the everyday things.

People said, *"He'll realize what he lost."*
Maybe he will, maybe he won't.
But I've realized what **I** lost —

the girl who kept saying "it's okay" even when it wasn't,
the girl who kept proving her worth to someone who
had already stopped looking.

Now I'm learning to be gentle with myself.
I buy flowers for my own room.
I take long showers, go for walks, eat dinner without
staring at my phone.
Some days, I even hum while folding clothes.
It's not happiness — not yet, but that's just enough for
now.

He once said, *"You take things too personally."*
Maybe.
But at least I felt things deeply —
and that's not weakness.
That's proof I loved honestly.

I'm not angry anymore.
I don't want him back either.
I just want to remember how to be myself again —
without shrinking, without waiting, without explaining.

Because he didn't just leave.
He took away the version of me that thought love was
enough.
And maybe that's how I'll remember him —

I'm just learning to breathe again,
in a world that feels a little emptier without him.

Chapter 4. Almost Love

He said, *"I care."*
But care without effort is just noise.
Love isn't supposed to be convenient —
it's supposed to be constant.

He'd call daily,
text whenever he gets time,
say *"love you"* like it cost nothing.
And I believed it,
because when you love someone,
you don't listen to tone —
you listen to hope.

Love didn't end with silence this time,
it ended with routine.
With the same words that once meant everything
but had no warmth left inside them.
He still asked how my day was,
but it felt like small talk,
not love.

It's strange —
when someone leaves, at least you know where to place the pain.

But when they stay and change,
you keep searching for what's missing,
as if love just misplaced itself somewhere between the calls.

I'd tell myself, *"He's trying."*
But you can feel it, right?
When the energy shifts.
When the same *"I miss you"* sounds forced.

He said, *"The vibes feel different."*
And I wanted to scream, *"Of course they do!"*
Because love isn't about vibes —
it's about effort, about showing up even when it's not perfect.
But how do you argue with a feeling?
You can't.
You just watch someone slowly detach,
while pretending everything's normal.

He didn't stop calling.
He just stopped meaning it.
And that's worse.
Because you start doubting your own heart —
wondering if you imagined the whole thing.

The hardest goodbyes are the ones

that never sound like goodbye at all.
The pain of almost love runs the deepest —
it doesn't end; it just becomes a part of you.

Chapter 5. When Love Feels Uncomfortable

Love had plans that week.
A suitcase open, a heart open wider.
And then, one small word changed it all.
Not anger, not distance
that somehow reached me too.

He said, *"I'm not feeling well."*
Fever. Weak. Exhausted.
And I said, *"It's okay, I'll come. I'll take care of you."*
Because that's what love is, right?
You show up when the world tires them out.

But he said, *"No... I'm uncomfortable. I don't want you to see me like this."*
Uncomfortable.
That one word changed everything.

I thought we were past that stage.
We had shared laughter, comfort, softness.
But maybe what felt safe to me
felt heavy to him.
Maybe he wasn't avoiding me —
maybe he was hiding from himself.

Sometimes people don't run from love,
they run from being seen.
And I think that night,
my care touched an old wound he wasn't ready to face.

I called him after a few hours.
He was watching a movie, eating dinner — calm,
ordinary.
As if nothing had cracked between us.
And I spoke like I wasn't breaking.
That's how love ends — not in fights,
but in voices that sound normal while hearts fall apart.

He was fine after a few days.
Laughing again, living again.
And I was still stuck in that moment,
replaying a word that ruined everything.
Uncomfortable —
funny how a feeling so small
can end something so big.

Chapter 6. It Was Just One Month

And so, I started to walk away — slowly, painfully —
but with the knowing that my love was never wasted,
my feelings were never wrong,
and I was never weak.

The hardest thing isn't love —
it's walking away with a heart still beating for someone who's gone.
And the most beautiful thing
isn't being loved back,
but learning to hold your own hand through the pain.

He once said, *"It was just one month... and you really started to love me."*
I froze for a moment.
How could I explain it?
How do you explain something that lives inside you,
something that feels bigger than yourself,
something only your heart understands.

He became my safe place without even trying.
Not because he was perfect,
but because he was real —

because for a while, he understood me without judgment.

But one month can change everything.
One month can hold a lifetime —
the first laugh, the last call,
and the silence that follows you everywhere.

I forgave myself for loving him with no limits,
for building dreams out of ordinary days,
for holding onto every word like it was a promise.
Because even love that isn't returned
still teaches the heart how to pray.

He couldn't understand.
Some people measure love in days,
others measure it in moments.
He measured it in time.
I measured it in heartbeat.

Love is something deeply your own —
no one can touch it, no one can take it away.
Even if someone walks out,
even if their heart doesn't echo yours,
it doesn't make your love smaller.
What you felt was real.
It was yours, and that's enough.

Maybe that's what closure truly means —
to forgive them,
to forgive yourself,
and to keep love alive inside you,
not for them anymore,
but as proof that your heart once knew how to stay.

Now, when I think of him,
it doesn't ache the same.
It just reminds me —
I once loved enough
to feel everything.
Even if it was just one month.

Chapter 7 . The Maybe Phase

No one talks about the phase after goodbye —
the one where you still type messages and erase them,
where you talk to them in your head
like they're still listening.
It's not love anymore,
but it's not nothing either.

You build a whole world with them in your mind —
the conversations you never had,
the apologies that never came,
the mornings that only existed in dreams.

I still talk to him in my head.
I tell him how my day was,
ask about his,
laugh at things he'd find funny.
It's madness, I know —
but it's the only way to keep him alive
without actually having him.

You want to forget him,
but a part of you refuses to.
Because you're still living in the talks, the dreams,

the half-finished plans that only exist in memory.
You don't want him —
you just don't know how to live
without the version of him your heart built.

That's what *maybe* is —
a conversation that never really ends.
Maybe he'll call.
Maybe he still thinks of me.
Maybe it was real.
Maybe I wasn't the only one feeling it.
Maybe he'll come back.
Maybe, maybe, maybe...

And that's how it eats you — quietly.
You stop living in reality
and start living in what could've been.
You don't move forward,
you just spin —
in circles, in questions, in love that still breathes.

You start losing it, you know?
You see them when they're not there.
You talk in your head because reality's too quiet.
You live inside scenes that never happened.
And that's how madness begins —

when love stops,
but refuses to leave.

Chapter 8 . Things I Didn't Say

You said you were uncomfortable.
That you didn't want me to see you like that — tired, weak, not yourself.
And I wanted to say, *"That's exactly when love is supposed to stay."*

I tried to explain, but you called it arguing.
I wasn't fighting you — I was fighting for you.
I stayed quiet because I didn't want to sound like pressure.
But what I never said was this —
it wasn't your fever that broke me,
it was how easily you pushed me away.

You said, *"I'm confused. I need space."*
And I waited.
Waited till time became silence,
and silence became absence.

You started calling less,
then not at all.
I kept reaching out,
thinking love meant not giving up.

But I learned — sometimes waiting
is just another way of breaking yourself quietly.

You called it space.
But space doesn't mean silence.
It's not vanishing and calling it peace.
It's not throwing someone away and naming it clarity.
Space means breathing apart, not breaking apart.

You left me there —
alone, waiting, confused.
I kept calling, just to hear you say,
"Why can't you understand? I'm confused. Give me space."
And I wanted to scream —
"This isn't space. It's just walking away, because you were just scared to be seen".

I cried — cried till my body gave up.
Tried to explain, tried to make you understand.
But you said, *"The vibes changed."*

Vibes changed… because that night,
you thought I was arguing.
I was trying to hold you while you were pushing me away.
You called it conflict,

I called it care that came out clumsy.
You heard noise,
I was just scared.

Days later, you asked for another chance.
And I believed you.
And then when I called, you said,
"You should move on. I told you I broke up."
As if all those words were never spoken,
as if hope was something I had imagined just to survive.

There's so much I didn't say.
How your silence humiliated me.
How waiting turned me into someone I no longer recognized.
How I kept forgiving you for things you never admitted to doing.

I want to tell you —
love doesn't need perfection,
it only needs presence.
But now, those words live somewhere between my chest and throat,
like ghosts that never learned how to leave.

It's strange —
I said nothing and still lost everything.

Chapter 9 . The Halfway Home

Halfway.
That's where I'm stuck —
between holding on and finally letting go.
I'm not waiting for him anymore,
but I still look back,
like my heart hasn't received the message my mind already read.

The truth is, I'm just tired of crying.
I've learned to hide my pain
inside routine, inside silence,
inside smiles that don't reach my eyes.

Now I sleep without that song he sang for me once.
Back then, I couldn't fall asleep without hearing it.
I must've played it a hundred times —
as if repeating it would bring him back.

There are small things I've stopped doing —
things that once made me feel close to him.
I don't check his city's weather anymore.
I don't keep the messages I used to reread every night.
I don't wear the perfume he said smelled like me.

I left something in his car that day.
Maybe he still keeps it,
or maybe it's lying somewhere forgotten,
or maybe he threw it away —
like everything else we promised to hold on to.
But now, I've stopped thinking about it too.
Maybe it's broken now —
just like us.

He used to say, *"You're mine. I'm never going to leave you."*
And I believed him.
Not because I was foolish,
but because he said it like truth,
and I wanted to live inside that sentence forever.

Now he's completing the travel list we made together —
the same cities, the same plans,
just without me.
And I wonder if he ever pauses,
just for a second,
to remember who dreamt it with him first.

It's strange, isn't it?
How people keep living the life you built with them in your head,

while you're still standing in the ruins,
trying to recognize yourself again.

Halfway — that's where I am.
Not where he left me,
but not where I thought I'd end up either.
I don't miss him like before,
but I still miss the person I was when he loved me.

And maybe that's what heartbreak really is —
not the loss of someone,
but the quiet death of who you used to be
when love still felt safe.

Halfway home —
not there yet,
but far enough to know
I'll make it someday.

Chapter 10 . Lessons I Didn't Ask For

Promises are not made to last forever.
They sound beautiful when said,
but sometimes they're only meant to break.
There's nothing like fairytales in real life —
just people trying, failing, and leaving halfway.

I never asked for these lessons.
I only wanted love — gentle, safe, real.

But love doesn't always stay.
Sometimes it comes just to show you what it feels like
to be seen once before being left again.

He taught me how silence can break a person.
How distance can sound gentle,
but still mean goodbye.
How someone can still say *"I care,"*
and still walk away the next moment.

Love doesn't need much —
just two hearts that don't give up at the same time.
You thought I was foolish, but I was real.
You were busy counting days,

while I was living every moment like forever.

Sometimes even months, even years,
don't turn into love —
they just become habits, attachments, comfort.
And sometimes, one month is enough
to make you feel everything.

What is love?
It's not about forever — it's about truth.
It's madness we keep calling beautiful.
It makes you weak, makes you strong,
and still leaves you asking *why.*

It's the one thing that ruins you,
and still feels like the only thing worth being ruined for.
I learned that loving someone doesn't mean they'll stay,
and losing them doesn't mean you stop loving.
Some feelings just learn to live without names.

I didn't want to learn all this.
But maybe love was meant to break me first,
just so I'd see what I'm made of.
Not everyone you hold will stay.
But everyone you love leaves a trace —
and sometimes that's all you get to keep.

Some stories don't end with closure,
they just stop — and you learn to live in the pause.
And now, I'm learning to live
without expecting fairytales,
without waiting for closure,
without needing someone to understand.

Chapter 11 . The Why That Never Ended

At first, I didn't believe it was over.
You can't lose something that loud so quietly, right?
I thought maybe he just needed time.
Maybe tomorrow he'd text.
Maybe next week he'd call.
Maybe he'd still remember the way I said his name.

I kept calling — not every hour, but enough for hope to survive.
Sent him reels, random texts,
as if one smile could fix everything that fell apart.
But silence has its own language —
and his said everything I didn't want to hear.

Why did you say you loved me, if you didn't mean to stay?
Why build a world with me, only to burn it quietly?
Why call every morning, text every night,
just to call it *vibes* in the end?

Why did you teach me how to feel safe,
and then make me question what love even means?
Why did you look at me like forever

and then vanish like it was nothing?

Why did you ask me to trust you,
then leave me holding promises that had no home?
Why did you say, *"I'm confused,"*
when all it needed was truth?

I asked everyone — my friends, my brother, my mom.
And every time they said, *"Maybe he wasn't ready,"*
I heard something else —
He was ready, just not for me.

I told my story to strangers too.
Like it belonged to someone else.
Like if I said it enough times,
I'd finally understand it.
But all I found were echoes —
my own voice, coming back unanswered.

He didn't just leave —
he broke me first,
scattered the pieces,
and then walked away like nothing happened.
And the worst part is,
I kept searching for the version of him that loved me once,
as if he was still hiding somewhere inside the silence.

Why do I still care?
Why does it still hurt, even now?
Why does my heart still whisper your name
like it doesn't know it's over?

And maybe that's the real *why* that never ends —
the one that doesn't look for answers anymore,
just learns to live inside the question.

Chapter 12 . If You Had Stayed, Maybe I'd Still Be Me

If you had stayed,
maybe I'd still be me.
The girl who laughed easily,
who danced in her room while getting ready,
who believed love meant safety, not survival.

Now, everything feels heavier —
songs, mornings, even breathing.
I wake up and don't know what to do with myself.
Nothing feels like mine anymore.
Not my room, not my reflection, not my heart.

Some days, I try to do things I used to love.
Make chai, light a candle, play music.
But even that feels like pretending.
I stare at my phone, scroll through old pictures,
and end up doing nothing.
It's like he left,
and took all my colors with him.

People tell me, *"You'll find yourself again."*

But what if I don't want to find her?
What if I just want the peace she had before him?
Before love became this exhausting thing —
a memory that hurts to touch,
but hurts even more to forget.

If you had stayed,
maybe I wouldn't be this tired.
Maybe I'd still laugh at small things,
still sing off-key,
still believe that goodbyes have reasons.
But you didn't.
And now, I'm left with a silence
that speaks louder than his voice ever did.

I'm not strong yet.
I'm just showing up — barely.
There are days I can't eat,
days I can't talk,
days I can't feel anything at all.
But I still wake up.
And maybe that counts for something.

Because deep down,
somewhere beneath the ruins,
I know I wasn't always this broken.
There was a girl before him —

whole, soft, unafraid.
And even if it takes everything in me,
I'll find her again someday.
Not today, not soon,
but someday.

And maybe that's the only hope I have left —
that I'll return to myself.
That I'll look in the mirror
and finally recognize the eyes staring back.
The girl who loved without fear,
the girl who still deserves peace.

Maybe she's waiting for me —
just like I once waited for him.

Chapter 13 . The Hardest Habit to Break

There's an art to not checking.
It doesn't come easily — it comes after nights of staring at the screen,
after typing a message and erasing it before you hit send,
after scrolling through his profile just to feel close again,
and ending up feeling emptier than before.

Scenario 1: The Door You Keep Knocking On
You keep his number saved,
not because you'll call,
but because deleting it feels like giving up hope.
You still follow him,
pretend it's casual — "just seeing how he's doing."
You see him laugh,
post,
travel —
and you feel it all over again.
Not the love — the loss.

You still go to his page,
scroll through pictures you've already seen a hundred times.

You look at who he follows,
who liked his picture,
who commented something sweet.
You don't double tap, you just stare.
You zoom in, you compare.
And after every scroll,
you feel smaller, quieter —
like you've built your own cage and forgot where the key is.

Checking doesn't heal you.
It only pulls you away from yourself.
Every scroll reopens what you're trying to close.
It doesn't make him miss you —
it only makes you forget yourself a little more.

Scenario 2: When You Choose Not to Check

One night, you finally unfollow him —
not for peace, not for closure,
but because anger felt easier than pain.
You tell yourself he'll notice.
He'll see it.
He'll ask, "Why did you unfollow me?"
Maybe he'll even send a request again,
just to remind you he still cares.

But he doesn't.

Days pass.
He doesn't notice.
He doesn't ask.
And that silence — that's what breaks you.
Because you realize,
you were never the absence he felt.

You stare at your phone,
looking at the same profile again and again.
You're the one who hit unfollow,
but somehow it still feels like he's the one who left again.
You want to follow him back,
just once — just to see if he'll notice, if he'll react.
But your hand stops mid-air.
Because deep down, you know —
this is what surviving looks like at first: messy, quiet, and lonely.

You didn't unfollow him to prove anything.
You did it because you were tired of losing yourself
in someone who wasn't even looking for you anymore.
You did it to protect your peace,
even when it felt like breaking your own heart.

I spoke for both sides —
for the one who still checks, and the one who finally stops.

But tell me this — does that make us fools
for loving deeply, for believing in men who promise forever?
Or does it only prove that men know how to play it well,
while women mistake honesty for love and end up
breaking themselves in it?

Because falling isn't foolish — it's human.
What's foolish is what men do —
feel everything, then walk away saying, "I'm just not feeling it anymore."
But I call it courage —
to love, to lose, and still survive.

Because whether you check or you don't, you still love —
just differently.

Chapter 14 . We're Not the Fools

We just loved louder than they were brave enough to stay.

To the men who left —
you always said you needed space.
No, you needed escape.
Because space is meant to breathe,
but you used it to disappear.

You called it confusion,
but confusion doesn't delete conversations.
Confusion doesn't ignore calls.
Confusion doesn't make you cold overnight.
That's not confusion — that's cowardice.

You said you cared,
but caring isn't selective.
You said you loved,
but love doesn't run every time it's asked to stay.
You said you were overwhelmed —
but the truth is, you were just never ready
for a woman who actually meant it.

You left because love felt like work,
and you only wanted the warmth — not the responsibility.
You left because she made you see yourself,
and you couldn't stand the reflection.

And still, somehow, *we* get called fools.

To the women who stayed —
you, who begged for clarity and were called dramatic.
You, who gave everything and were told you gave too much.
You are not weak — you were *real.*
You stayed, not because you couldn't leave,
but because you believed in something men have forgotten — effort.

You waited, not for him,
but for the version of love he promised you.
You loved deeply, and that doesn't make you a fool.
It makes you alive in a world full of emotionally dead men.

Stop apologizing for caring too much.
Stop blaming yourself for being the one who stayed.
You didn't lose him — he lost someone who would've never left.

And to every man who walks away saying, *"I'm just not feeling it anymore,"*
remember this —
you don't get to call it honesty when it's actually escape.
You don't get to break something pure
and call it "not the right vibe."

To the women —
stop giving up on yourself so easily.
You are not something to recover from,
you are the storm he couldn't handle.
You are the closure he'll search for in every next girl.
You are not foolish for staying —
you are brave for surviving love that didn't know how to stay.

Chapter 15 . Maybe This Was What I Needed

If you remember —
Chapter 10 was *Lessons I Didn't Ask For*.
Back then, I was all questions —
angry, loud, restless.
I kept shaking the sky for answers
that were never meant to fall.

But now, after everything you've read,
after everything I've felt,
Maybe this — all of it — was what I needed.

Because every heartbreak is a classroom
that doesn't warn you when the lesson begins.
You walk in with love,
you walk out with truth.

And when it's finally quiet,
you ask, *what now?*
After the tears, the silence, the looping thoughts?
After the nights you whispered their name
into an empty phone screen?

When the heart breaks, light enters.

It's ugly, but it's real.
And maybe both are right,
How pain breaks you open
Just enough for truth to enter.

You stop looking for closure —
because sometimes, closure isn't a message or an apology,
it's just exhaustion.
It's realizing you've run out of ways to fix something that doesn't want to be repaired.

So you start doing small things.
You water the plant you almost let die —
the one that dried up the week he left.
You change your bedsheet —
because maybe new sheets will help you sleep.
You make tea and drink it alone —
without checking your phone,
without waiting for "good morning."
You reply to that friend you kept ignoring,
because talking feels heavy,
but silence feels worse.
You smile at a stranger,
and then wonder when was the last time you actually meant it.
You laugh at something silly,

then stop midway — because it feels strange to be happy again.
But it's okay.
That's how it begins — quietly.

But that's how it starts — quietly.
Not in big moments,
but in tiny, tired acts of trying.
You wake up one morning
and realize your first thought wasn't about them.
And that hits harder than any goodbye —
because it means you're healing,
even if you didn't mean to.

And that's what comes after.
Not peace that's loud or proud,
but peace that simply sits beside you,
breathing quietly, saying — *You survived. You stayed.*

Maybe he wasn't the forever I wanted.
Maybe he was the reason I learned
how to love myself louder than anyone else ever could.
Maybe I didn't ask for these lessons,
but I think I finally understand them.
He was never the ending —
he was just the ache
that taught me how to begin again.

Chapter 16 . Not Everything That Feels Like Love Is Love

Love is not a cage; it is the wind.
Then why do we keep locking ourselves in?
Maybe both are right.
Because what we often call love —
is sometimes just attachment...
and sometimes only a habit.

We all think it's love — until it starts hurting more than healing.
We dress it up with words like forever, comfort, destiny —
but most of the time,
it's not love at all.
It's something that looks like it,
feels like it,
but breaks us in ways love never should.

What I felt had many names,
but only one truth —
not everything that feels like love is love.

So come with me for a moment.
Let's see what love really is —

through my eyes, through my scars.
Maybe you'll find your own story hiding somewhere in mine.

1. Love
Love doesn't always give you butterflies — sometimes it gives you peace.
The real kind doesn't make your heart race; it makes it rest.

You know what love really is?
It's not the 3 a.m. texts or constant calls.
It's not needing each other every second.
It's when they don't reply for hours,
and you still trust them.
It's when you don't have to remind them who you are —
because love remembers, even in silence.

People think love is about merging.
But no — love is walking side by side,
with your own dreams, your own fears,
and still choosing to stay connected.

Love isn't when someone says, *"You're mine."*
It's when they look at you and you just know —
you belong, even without words.

Real love isn't dramatic.
It's peace that still feels like warmth.
It's arguments that don't end with blocking,
but with one small message — *"I'm still here."*

It's knowing that what's real doesn't need chasing.
It's remembering the chai order,
saving the last bite of dessert — not out of habit,
but out of love.

Love doesn't need grand gestures or forever promises.
It's ordinary, quiet, consistent —
and that's what makes it rare.

Because real love never says *"mine."*
It just stays — calmly, like it was always meant to.

2. Attachment
Attachment always looks like love at first.
It starts beautifully — like butterflies when they text first,
when their name lights up your screen and your world
suddenly softens.

That feeling feels like magic —
but it isn't always love.
It's just your fear wearing perfume,
your heart mistaking attention for affection.

You check your phone every few minutes.
You wait for their replies like oxygen.
You replay conversations, reread old chats,
search for clues that they still care.

You call it love —
but love doesn't make you restless.
It makes you steady.

Attachment whispers, *"I can't live without you."*
Love whispers, *"I'll miss you, but I'll survive."*

With attachment, you stop recognizing yourself.
You start revolving your day around their mood.
You cancel plans, lose sleep,
make excuses for their silence.

You think if you love them harder, they'll stay.
But they don't.
Because attachment doesn't hold — it clings.

Attachment isn't love.
It's fear pretending to be devotion.
It's the ache of needing constant proof.
And one day, when you finally stop checking your phone,

you'll realize —
you weren't addicted to them.
You were addicted to the feeling of being seen.

3. Habit

Habit is the quietest heartbreak of all.
It doesn't scream anymore — it just lingers.
It's not chaos; it's emptiness.
And that's what makes it dangerous.

It starts after they've already gone,
but your days still orbit around their memory.
You wake up and check your phone —
not for them, but because your hands still remember how.

You scroll through Instagram,
not because you care anymore,
but because checking became your routine.

You play the same songs,
stand in front of the mirror,
remember the way they once said your name.
That's habit —
not missing them,
just missing the pattern of having them.

It's when you still type their name,
then erase it before sending.
You don't love them anymore —
you just don't know how to stop remembering.

Habit doesn't break you — it dulls you.
It doesn't hurt loud — it hurts every day, quietly.
And the only way to end it
is to replace it.

Walk, work, breathe, live —
even when it feels mechanical.
Because one morning,
you'll reach for your phone,
and realize you weren't checking for them.
You were just checking the time.

That's when you know —
the habit broke before you did.

And after all this — the love, the attachment, the habit —
you start to wonder what any of it really was.

Love frees you.
Attachment traps you.
Habit consumes you.
And the only way to know the difference

is to lose all three once.

Because that's how you learn —
what was real, what was need,
and what was never love at all.

Chapter 17. I Still Text Only for Validation

Sometimes we don't miss the person — we miss the way their attention made us feel real.

I still text him sometimes.
Not because I want him back,
but because I want to know I still exist somewhere in his story.
It's not love anymore —
just a quiet way of asking, *"Do you still remember me, or was it always just me?"*

It's strange, isn't it?
How after a breakup, we still reach out.
We don't want them back,
we just want to know we weren't that easy to forget.
We text hoping for one small sign — a reply, a word, a mcmory
anything that makes us feel like what we had was real.

I tell myself, *"It's just one text, it's harmless."*
But deep down, I know I'm not looking for a conversation —
I'm looking for proof that I still matter.

And that's what validation does —
it makes you mistake temporary attention for healing.

Sometimes he replies.
A short, dry message —
"yeah," "sure," "been busy."
And for a second, I feel something — relief maybe.
But it fades as quickly as it comes.
Because no text, no reply,
can fill the space he left behind.

We do this because silence feels unbearable.
Because it's hard to accept that someone you gave everything to
can just move on like you were never there.
We text because we want to feel seen,
even if it's by the person who broke us.

But here's the truth —
every time you text him for validation,
you teach your heart to settle for crumbs.
You tell yourself that being noticed is enough,
when what you really deserve is to be chosen.

The reply you're waiting for —
it won't heal you.

It'll only remind you of the distance between what was and what will never be again.

One day, you'll stop reaching out.
Not because you hate him,
but because you'll be tired of proving your worth
to someone who couldn't see it when you gave him everything.

And when that day comes,
you'll finally understand —
you never needed his reply to feel enough.
You were enough even when the chat said *"seen."*

Yes, you made him your everything — your story, your reason, your home.
And now you're learning to live in the ruins he left behind.
But listen — homes can be rebuilt,
and stories can be rewritten.
This time, let the story begin with *you.*

Chapter 18 . You're Not Lonely, You're Just Out of Practice

After a breakup, silence becomes your best friend — and your worst enemy.
You wake up and check your phone, knowing there's nothing there.
You talk to yourself in your head, replay conversations like a ritual.
You start depending on your own voice because his is gone.
You ask the mirror questions it never answers.
You scroll through old chats just to remember how it felt to be seen.
That's not love anymore — that's survival.

You stop going out.
You stop replying to friends.
You cancel plans with excuses like "I'm tired" when really, you're just afraid to exist without him.
And in the quiet, you start believing that maybe this is who you are now —
someone people left, someone who doesn't belong anywhere.

But here's the truth —
you're not lonely, you're just out of practice.
You've been talking to ghosts for so long that you forgot
how real people sound.
You forgot what it's like to laugh and mean it.
You forgot that there are worlds outside your pain.

"Don't stay where you're needed only as a memory."
"Enough. Get up. Take a shower. Stop scrolling his
profile. Go meet your friends. The world didn't end — he
just walked out of it."

So, start small.
Text that one friend you ghosted when you fell in love.
Go out — even if you don't know what to say.
Sit in cafes.
Watch people.
Let life touch you again.
You don't have to trust everyone — just start showing
up.
Because healing doesn't come from solitude.
It comes from belonging again.

Some nights, you'll still come home and talk to yourself,
because no one else feels safe yet — and that's okay.
You'll cry, and it'll still sting,

but the ache will start to have a shape you can live with.
You'll realize — it's not that you don't have people,
it's that you stopped reaching for them when you lost
him.

So, stop waiting for him to text.
Stop talking to yourself like you're the problem.
Stop thinking you're hard to love.
You're not.
You just gave all your love to someone who didn't know
what to do with it.

And now it's time — to give it back to yourself,
and maybe, one day,
to someone who won't make you beg to be seen.

Because loneliness isn't romantic.
It's just another word for forgetting how to begin again.
And maybe you're not broken —
you're just learning how to live again,
how to laugh again,
how to belong again —
with the world, with people, with yourself.

Chapter 19. The Only Way Out Is Through

Miracles don't exist.
No one wakes up one morning suddenly healed.
No text magically arrives saying, "I miss you."
No closure appears out of thin air.
You just get tired —
of crying, of checking, of waiting.
And that's when real change begins.
You stop praying for him to come back
 and start praying for your mind to finally rest.
Because after heartbreak, there are only two ways to live —

Scenario 1: The Days You Stay Still
You sit on your bed all day,
scrolling through reels you don't remember watching.
You keep the curtains closed,
tell yourself you need rest,
but the truth is — it's not rest, it's escape.

You eat to fill the silence,
snack after snack, bite after bite,
until the ache dulls but never leaves.
You tell yourself you'll go to the gym tomorrow,

that you'll clean your room "later."
But later never comes.
The dishes pile up,
your reflection looks unfamiliar,
and your heart grows heavier — not from love,
but from everything you've stopped doing.
Because pain, when fed with comfort,
only grows hungrier.

Scenario 2: The Days You Fight Back
And then, there are the other days —
the ones where you get up anyway.
You make your bed, even if your hands shake.
You shower, even if it feels pointless.
You put on clean clothes,
not to impress anyone — just to feel human again.
You play music,
loud enough to make your thoughts quiet.
You go for a walk,
you cook,
you clean,
you show up — not because you're over him,
but because you've decided to start choosing you.

That's the secret no one tells you —
you don't heal by forgetting him.
You heal by remembering yourself.

You learn that miracles don't come from wishing;
they come from movement.
From the hundred small choices you make every day —
to not text,
to not check,
to not crumble again.

And yes, you'll still think of him sometimes.
In the middle of your workday,
in the silence after dinner.
But it won't tear you apart anymore.
The thought will come —
and then go —
like background noise in a house that's finally your own
again.

One day, you'll lie down at night, exhausted —
and realize you were too busy to miss him.
Not healed, not over it —
just tired enough to let peace walk in.

That's how it happens —
not through miracles,
but through minutes that pile up
until the ache forgets how to be loud.

So if you can't forget him yet,

don't.
Just get up.
Do the next thing.
Because the only way out of pain
is through it — step by step, day by day.

Chapter 20 . The Last Text You'll Never Send

This is for the ones still stuck —
still checking their phones,
still typing his name just to erase it again.
For the ones who tell themselves they're over it,
but still look at the moon and wonder if he's thinking of them too.

You keep running him in your head, don't you?
Every laugh, every word, every almost.
You replay what you could've said differently,
as if love ended because you missed a sentence.
You wake up thinking maybe he'll text.
You scroll his profile, looking for signs —
some post, some song, some story —
anything that says, *he remembers me too.*

But listen.
You can't heal while waiting for someone else to notice you're broken.
You can't move forward when your heart still lives where you were left.

We've all been there —

writing long unsent paragraphs,
crying in drafts,
turning pain into poetry,
as if art could make him return.
You convince yourself he'll realize it one day,
that love like yours can't be replaced.
But he already has — not you, but the version of himself
that needed you.

So, stop begging for closure in people who never wanted
to understand you.
Stop performing strength for someone who never stayed
long enough to see your softness.
Stop explaining how to love you right —
the right one will just know.

And I know, right now it feels impossible.
You can't imagine waking up without thinking of him.
You can't imagine laughter that doesn't feel borrowed.
But you will.
One day, he'll cross your mind,
and you won't feel pain — just peace.
You'll realize you weren't remembering him anymore —
you were remembering who you were when you loved
him.

Don't rush to forget.

Just promise yourself you'll keep living — even with the ache.
Because healing doesn't mean deleting him,
it means remembering yourself louder.

And to every girl reading this —
stop sending essays to prove your worth.
Stop explaining why you deserved better.
You don't need to write 250 lines to beg someone to treat you right.
The one who wants to stay will never make you ask twice.

So tonight, when your fingers itch to text him —
don't.
Close your eyes.
Let him go softly.
And remember this —
you were never hard to love.
He was just too small to hold something this real.

Because one day, you'll realize —
you never needed his reply to feel enough.
You just needed to come back to yourself.
And that's where love truly begins again.

Chapter 21 . It's Not You, It's Me (But It Was Always You)

This is for every man who left
with those same recycled words —
"It's not you, it's me."
"You deserve better."
"I just need to be sure."

You wanted her love,
but not her depth.
You wanted her warmth,
but not her truth.
You wanted to be loved —
just not held accountable for it.

You said you needed space.
No, you needed escape.
You said, "I'm not ready."
But you were ready enough to say *I love you* in 24 hours
just not ready to mean it 24 days later.

And when she cried,
you called it "too much."

When she stayed,
you called it "pressure."
When she tried to understand,
you said, "You're overthinking."
You made her believe that her love was heavy —
but the truth is,
you were just too fragile to carry something real.

Men like you turn "forever" into a phase,
and then post reels about "healing energy" and "focusing on myself,"
while the woman you broke is sitting on the floor,
staring at her phone,
trying to make sense of a love that vanished mid-sentence.

You move on in silence.
She breaks in public.
You distract yourself with the gym, work, noise —
she rewatches old messages, cries into her pillow,
scrolls through heartbreak reels that sound too familiar.

Because that's what happens —
when men leave, they disappear.
When women love, they stay even after being left.
She'll tell herself it's okay.
She'll make excuses for you.

She'll replay every moment, searching for what she missed.
You'll sleep fine.
She won't.

And yet, she'll still rise.
She'll go to work with puffy eyes,
smile at people who don't know how much she's holding back.
She'll sit in traffic,
hear your favorite song,
and for a second — it'll all come rushing back.
But this time, she won't text.
She won't explain.
She'll just keep driving.
Because one day, she'll realize —
she was never asking for too much.
You were just offering too little.

So, to all the men who say,
"It's not you, it's me."
Maybe, for once, stop running.
Stop testing good women just to prove your brokenness.
Stop calling love *pressure*
when it's just accountability dressed in honesty.

And to every woman reading this —

you were never too much.
You were just too real for someone who was pretending to feel.
You were not the mistake —
you were the lesson he'll never admit he needed.

Because love was never supposed to be about timing —
it was about choosing.
And he didn't choose you.
But you — you still chose love.
Even when it hurt.
Even when it left.
Even when it said, "It's not you."

So no, it wasn't you.
But it was never really him either —
just a man who mistook intensity for love,
and fear for freedom.

And one day, when he scrolls through another heartbreak reel,
he'll see a line that sounds too familiar —
and he'll pause.
Not because he misses you,
but because he finally knows
he'll never find that kind of love twice.

From the Author

If you've reached this far, thank you — truly.

If any page made you pause,
if any line felt like something you once lived —
I'd love to hear from you.
Your stories, your thoughts, your maybes —
they're the reason this book exists.

You can write to me at:
 miss.tiramisu.writes@gmail.com

Maybe together, we'll write the next chapter —
one that doesn't end in heartbreak,
but begins with healing.

With love,
– Miss Tiramisu

www.ingramcontent.com/pod-product-compliance
Lightning Source LLC
Chambersburg PA
CBHW060349050426
42449CB00011B/2886